AN INTRODUCTION TO THE ART OF PRESALES

Breaking the barriers of entry into sales engineering through empathy, creativity and change

Dr Tuuli Bell, PhD

Tuuli Bell Ltd

Omistettu Marille

CONTENTS

Title Page

Copyright

Dedication

Preface

Part 1: Introduction   1

Introduction   3

The role of presales: When and why is a presales consultant   7
needed?

Presales in B2B transactions   10

Core skills and paths into presales   14

What you might be surprised to learn   18

Supporting the salesperson, and the sales process   24

Technical wizard a.k.a. customer's trusted advisor   29

Qualities of a great presales consultant   33

What makes a good presales consultant?   36

Why are some people naturally good at presales?   40

Self-awareness: do you know yourself?   43

Story about imposter syndrome   46

Part 2: Sales   47

A very short introduction to sales   48

Sales methodologies   50

Sales process   53

Sales from a legal perspective   58

Marketing fundamentals   61

Part 3: Sharing your wisdom   65

Sustainable presales is the future of presales   66

Updating internal process documentation and tools   70

Making your efforts visible and reusable by the rest of the   73
organisation

Thanks   77

About The Author   79

Books In This Series   81

Acronyms: sales, organisation and technology related   85

Words explained   91

Closing remarks   93

PREFACE

So much of writing a book is timing. This book goes much beyond the spring of 2021 during which it was created; the idea has lingered for several years. I had a long break at Christmas, as so many of us did during the pandemic. I was reflecting on the year about to end. It had been my first full year of trading, my first year as a Founder and CEO, and it hadn't exactly gone to plan. A worldwide pandemic had hit within months of setting up my business. All that I had worked for seemed to have vanished overnight with the announcement of lockdown.

I had started establishing a client-base, to help sales directors reach their target by finding out what doesn't work in their sales process and collectively finding solutions to their problems. My problem was that I had done all this work in face-to-face workshops, and in my view, face to face could never be replicated in a virtual environment.

It didn't take long for the ripple-effect of fear and uncertainty spread from citizens to B2C, to B2B like the ones I worked with. Uncertainty is not seen as a great thing in business and I soon was back to square one, with only one remaining customer.

After the dust had settled, I was back into the world of business, but not as I knew it. Whereas previously companies were happy with building and developing their long-term sales strategies with my help, now they wanted immediate return on their investment. I was asked to create sales templates that could be used straight-away, write customer-specific documents that would be key to closing an on-going sale, and collate answers to hundreds of questions that could stop a sale from happening.

Then, at Christmas, it hit me. Most of my income had come from doing presales consulting, and I loved it.

I knew I wanted to write a book, and now was the time. I asked my old manager for his opinion, and being more than supportive of the idea, I launched into making a plan. There is no time like the present and I had time before my next contract was going to start.

But I needed more help and wanted to ensure that this book would benefit those who read it. I joined a community of presales consultants and received a warm welcome. Talking through what problem existed that the book could solve, it became increasingly clear that there's a lack of guidance for people who want to join a presales team, whether temporarily or permanently.

I would seen this happen throughout my career, and increasingly in the past year: companies still wanted to grow but were hesitant to hire costly presales consultants. The companies then ended up asking anyone who is available, to help with documents, demonstrations and sales conversations that had a technical aspect. When the task is finished, or help no longer required, the helper is sent back to their normal work which is often post-sale consulting, product management or product support. The cycle then repeats itself during the next sale opportunity.

Generally there is little support, help or training, and the new team members are thrown to the deep-end with varying success. Not only is it a costly way for companies to do business, jeopardizing a sale, but also can hit the confidence of the employee if they fail in their task.

If you've ever been in a situation described above, this book is for you. I believe that anyone, with the right tools, guidance, and an open mind, can be great at presales. I am honoured to serve as your guide as we discover the art of presales together.

PART 1: INTRODUCTION

The role of presales

INTRODUCTION

Solve real business problems. Find a technical solution. Be at the heart of the most complex sales operations. Influence the product roadmap. Wow the customer during a demonstration. Produce best-in-class visuals. Speak at international conferences. Share your vision at exclusive roundtables. Earn a great salary.

Sounds like your dream come true? Get ready for your adventure as a brand-new ... presales consultant!

Figure 1: The presales roles is one of the most varied roles and combines sales and technical skills. You will need to be able to think, and pause, on the spot.

Just like the job description, the presales profession is varied with different names, but do not let it put you off from this wonderful, often lesser-known profession. All these names refer to the same position: a person who is working as part of the sales team, but with deep technical insight. Some of the names include: sales engineer, presales architect, solutions consultant, solutions architect, sales support engineer, SE, SC, systems engineer, technical sales consultant, and trusted advisor.

It is now almost nine years since I started in my first presales consultancy role. I wasn't at first sure about what it was, but I was lucky to have a knowledgeable manager who had time to train me and had patience in my developing skills. At the organization that I work at the time, we had a great program for new joiners, and I was given additional freedom to take courses that helped me find the skills within me to become a great presales advisor.

At the heart of it, presales is about creating a world that the customer wants to buy. You are there because you are the customer's technical expert, a trusted advisor who guides them through sometimes a very difficult procurement process. One of the biggest differences between post sale and presales consultant is that the presales consultant is part of the sales team. Further, that mean that a presales consultant can have very lucrative bonuses. There are risks, of course. You are at the heart of sales operations which means that quarterly business reviews will soon become a regular checkpoint in your life and in your job. You will be measured against your technical ability, but you will also be dealing with clients who are the most demanding in terms of business requirements. Because they are under a lot of pressure from their own companies, your contact with the ultra-demanding customers can also be emotionally taxing and rewarding.

You will be working with technology that is more advanced than what is needed by an average customer who require no or a little presales support.

As will be clear from this book, presales consultants have no specific degree as a prerequisite, and most have landed in presales by a happy accident. So whatever profession you are in right now I will help you find and identify the gaps in your knowledge and guide you through the entrance to the world of presales.

Let me clarify the intention of the book, by telling you a personal story that has shaped the way I see the world. Throughout my entire career, all the way back to my school years, I have mostly worked in a male-dominated, white, middle-class environment. To me, teams with limited diversity backgrounds limit the possibilities of science, technology, and culture. Not that I haven't liked working with my colleagues: I have really enjoyed my career so far. However, the customers, the citizens of this world, will benefit from a much wider, more representative sales force than what is most organisations currently have. There should be no reason for such lack of diversity. Thus, I invite everyone who is interested in technology, sales and creativity to consider the career path of a presales consultant.

You may wish to skip some sections of the book, however I intend to keep the reading light-hearted and enjoyable so that you would rather read the whole book. I will talk quite a bit about how you and the customer might be feeling at various stages, because if you can recognise how you feel it can really make a huge difference to the success of selling.

My personal vision is to bring joy to the world. I truly believe that we can make the world a better, more inclusive and more joyous place by opening the doors of presales to a much wider audience.

Let's get started!

Ps. At the end of each chapter, I've included more resources for you to explore. They will include books, videos and infographics which I've found particularly useful.

Pps. For ease of use, the references are also available on via the QR code below (which takes you to https://www.tuulibell.com/art-of-presales-references.html).

THE ROLE OF PRESALES: WHEN AND WHY IS A PRESALES CONSULTANT NEEDED?

Let me tell you a story about chocolate, and you will be able to remember the key learnings from this chapter easier. And yes, it is a business-related story, and it is about to get personal.

You want to buy some chocolate for your work friend. You could call them a colleague I suppose, but I always prefer the term work friend instead. It sets a precedence: you wouldn't want to hurt the feelings of a work friend, and you want them to be happy. Happy work friend, happy me. Sounds childish? Put it to work and try out for yourself. So, you go to a shop and buy a box of chocolates and hand it over. But you didn't know their vegan! Oh no. I was at my first meeting with the customer, felt ashamed for not getting the right stuff and asked if their partner might like them instead, to which he replied "Of course".

Figure 2: I like to bring vegan chocolates to business meetings to lift up the energies and build a human connection. It makes me happy, too, a win-win.

Why did I bring chocolates to a business meeting, you might rightly inquire? Quite simple, really. Time is precious and most business meetings can be lovely conversations, where you open up about your worries, exchange ideas, and make a plan until the next time you meet. I increase the odds of a positive meeting, as good quality chocolate simply lifts the energies in the room and at least you have an icebreaker, and you find a thing or two about the other person.

After my 'I am vegan' life-learning, I now opt for vegan chocolates if I am not absolutely sure the person is not vegan. There are people who do not like chocolate, of course, but they're in the minority, and even then, they will appreciate your gesture. I often buy mine from Hotel Chocolat in Paddington, walk in and ask the sales assistant what they would recommend.

For future reference, the chocolate buying process above is a so-called business-to-consumer (B2C) sale where I bought an 'off-the-shelf' product.

PRESALES IN B2B TRANSACTIONS

In a similar fashion, businesses buy products from other businesses. A big part of today's businesses only sell to businesses. These are called business-to-business (B2B) transactions. The reason for selling to businesses rather than individuals is money. It is not necessarily that individuals have less money to spend (although that's also true in most cases) but it is the way the money is allocated and measured. Let's walk through an example. If you expense a shiny new ergonomic chair for your bad back, and your boss signs it off, it is not as if your boss actually gives you the cash from her purse to go and buy one. It simply comes off from her budget, or better yet an organization-wide IT budget that seems to never end.

On the other hand, if you bought the expensive chair as 'yourself', you would have purchased it with money that you would already paid income tax on and worked hard to have that money in your bank account in the first place.

See what I mean about caring about money differently?

In this book we'll talk about technology sales, but the same principles could be applied to retail, or other lines of business. You may need some creative thinking but I am confident it is within your skillset.

Businesses will need special software, or technology that is made unique to them. This is what we call a configurable or a customisable product. Let's use an IT Service Management (ITSM) solution as an example. An ITSM tool is used by your company's IT team when you call them. Which, let's face it, we've all done when we are desperate for help right now, because we left it too late ("I need to wait how long to fix my long overdue laptop issue?"). The ITSM tool that your IT team uses might be visible to you, in which case you can access an internal portal. The portal could be named something funky like 'Employee Experience Site', 'Intranet' or a humble 'Service Catalog'. (If you are one of my ITSM friends, I apologise for the inaccurate use of the term Service Catalog.)

It is fairly understandable that when buying a new ITSM tool, a specially trained salesperson is needed who can understand the customer and their unique requirements. What makes the sales-person's job even more complex is that the customer might not actually know exactly what they need because of where they are coming from: the customer is buying something new because they want to do things differently. This is where a presales per-son comes in: as a presales consultant, you need to find what that 'different' means. In other words, you need to find out what the customer needs and wants, and then create a solution that the customer can adopt and afford.

In the case of an ITSM solution, you as a presales consultant would challenge if the customer really needs all functionality replicated in the new solution as was requested. As the presales consultant, you might advice the customer: "I might suggest changing some of your ITSM processes to the latest recommended framework of ITIL 4. This would bring additional value to the business by for example simplifying the purchasing of IT equipment. Your employ-ees would get a shiny new portal, too." Of course, you would want to steer them towards the out-of-the-box (OOTB) solution where feasible, because upgrades and future changes to software will be much easier. Win-win.

A presales consultant will work in conjunction with a salesperson and the technical experts within the company and create a solution that is custom-made for a particular customer. In other words, you are creating a world that the customer wants to buy.

As a side note, you may wish to challenge the 'custom-made' thesis and say "Hey, we have a presales team, and we sell off-the-shelf products". Yes, that's correct in some cases. But even in those cases, you as a presales consultant will help the customer choose which off-the-shelf products they would need to buy. You would guide the customer through the purchasing process from selecting from the options, influencing the decision, and overseeing the final sale.

lynch pin

One of the best metaphors I've heard about presales is a lynch pin. The story is courtesy of an old sales manager of mine, who spoke to me about it as an introduction to his team. The sale of the ITSM solution is a vehicle that needs to get from A to B, to close a sale. The salesperson is the engine, the one that pushes the vehicle, the sale, forwards. The other teams; post-sales consultants, service desk teams, and back office teams are the contents of the vehicle. Finally, the presales team is the lynch pin that holds the vehicle together; without it, you have the contents and the engine but the power from the engine isn't transferred to the wheels and the vehicle is stuck.

So far, we've clarified how the presales consultant is part of the sales team but has a distinct role from that of the salesperson, but it is also distinct from the role of the post-sale technical consultant. If it is neither a technical role, nor a sales role, how do you end up in presales? Let's take a closer look at paths into presales in the following chapter.

More resources to explore on...

...lynch pins:

[Video] Presales consultants are like lynch pins – holding the sales process together. Get inspired by those small, simple and important things in this video: https://www.youtube.com/watch?v=IUwzERG4EMY

CORE SKILLS AND PATHS INTO PRESALES

Speak to any presales consultant and you will find as many routes into the presales world as many people you will speak to. You will see people from post-sale consultancy roles, support teams, sales teams, even fresh out of university. What connects almost all presales consultants is that they found the role by accident and fell in love.

Let me share my story. In school, I had a great physics teacher. He said if you study physics you can become anything you want. I thought that's what I wanted to do: I want to be able to do anything. I was ambitious in my studies and I was determined to complete a PhD within six years of starting my undergraduate university course. It took me seven years, but still, not bad.

When I finished my PhD at the University of Cambridge, I knew I wanted to be part of something that had applications in real life, something in commercial and technology. If I would known presales back then, I might as well have chosen it as my career. For better or worse, I did not have that insight into the industry. It was a CEO of a thriving services organisation that had an extensive graduate programme who recognised my potential. He asked me to consider the role as a presales consultant, explaining that it is a challenging role but I would be able to learn it by working hard and using my initiative. I thought it sounded splendid.

The skills that you need as a presales consultant are closely related to the paths that you can take to be successful in your new presales role. I encourage you to visualise, throughout this chapter and the book, how you will feel, act, and behave in your new role. When you start with the end in mind, you are making a plan for positive change. At the end of this chapter, I have compiled some of my favourite business books for you to explore, also on the subject of 'Beginning with the end in mind'.

It is a mixture of things that you need as a presales consultant. Most importantly, you will need sales skills, technical skills and industry expertise. You will need to *creatively* and *empathetically* use those skills in harmony. Then, you will be a presales superstar. You do not need a university degree, unless you want one. What you need is a collection of skills and the ability to apply them in real life dynamic interactive complex scenarios. When you have passion, you will never grow tired of learning new things, creating new solutions, and thriving in new environments.

The collection of skills that you will need means that you can enter the presales world from lots of different backgrounds and be successful. For example, you might be a member of the sales team, and take technical training before joining the presales team. Or you might be a customer or a user of a software solution, and join the software company as a presales consultant. You'd then be able to empathise with prospective customers easily and build rapport by sharing how you benefited from the solution. Yet another point of entry could be a support team member who has a passion to both solve problems and create solutions. You will be able to learn the missing sales skills through shadowing, mentoring and sales training.

Figure 3: Paths into presales. To get into presales, you can start either in a sale role or a technical role. As you progress in your career, you can add the missing skills to your armour, and join a presales team.

In short, if you are new to presales, you would want to either (1) acquire product knowledge first, then learn sales, or (2) go by the sales route so as to speak the language of the customer first and then learn the product. You can learn the product in a number of teams such as software development, product, professional services, or customer success teams. You can learn the art of sales in teams like marketing, sales, partner management and business development.

Take a moment to reflect where you are right now, and where your next milestone is. What skills will you need in order to get there?

More resources to explore on...

...beginning with the end in mind:

[Book] The Secret by Rhonda Byrne https://www.thesecret.tv/products/the-secret-book/
[Book] 7 Habits of Highly Effective People by Stephen R. Covey https://www.franklincovey.com/the-7-habits/
[Book] Unapologetically Ambitious by Shellye Archambeau https://shellyearchambeau.com/books

WHAT YOU MIGHT BE SURPRISED TO LEARN

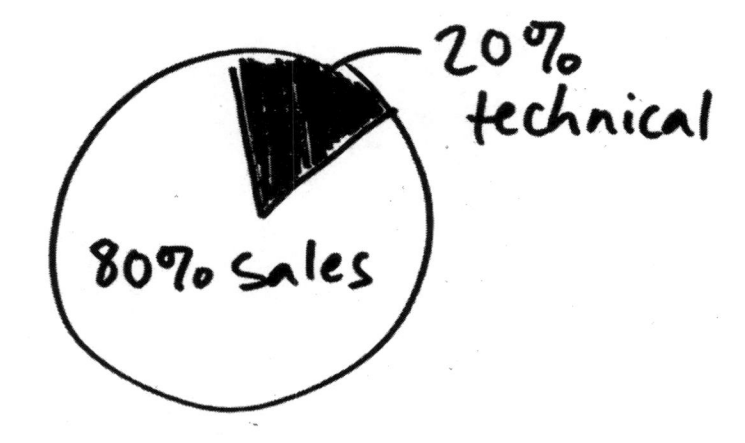

Figure 4: A common early misconception is that presales is dominated by technology. In reality, a successful presales consultant will need their sales skills a lot more than their technical skills.

Let's start this section with a diagram. Take a look at Figure 4. It shows everything I want to tell you in the section so if you are really in a hurry skip this one and go onto the next. However, if you would like to hear a story about how I transformed from a "technology-first" scientist into a management consultant that specialises in presales, read on.

As a matter of fact, what I am going to share with you, is also one of the few things that I have discussed with my brother about work. He and I do not talk about work very much. We should probably talk more in general, but that's another thing. We both agreed that technology without application is a waste. Think about that for a moment. If someone had told me that when I started as a physics undergraduate years ago, I would've said that's wrong. I would've said (and most likely did): "Well it is their problem if they do not get technology". What a cliché, but as I've become older and more experienced, I realised that it is so much more about the human being, about the user of technology than about the technology itself.

I think about my gran in Finland, in a care home on her own. She has an iPad, access to Internet, and a mobile phone. But she never answers her iPad, and we rarely speak. Why? It is not because she's incapable of learning things (she is very bright – turning ninety years this year, she is still publishing books). I believe it is because ultimately, there's a perception by my gran that the iPad is difficult to operate, and the iPad probably on silent and/or out of battery most of the time. So, how do her technical devices benefit her, if at all?

As a presales consultant, your role is to ensure that your customers are buying the right solution. There's two parts to it: Buying, and the solution. Whoever sold the iPad to my gran, got the buying part right, and possibly the solution as well, but forgot to train the customer.

What might be quite surprising to you, is what has got many of us in the field by surprise: A presales person is predominantly a salesperson who has technical expertise rather than the other way around. It is not a 50:50 split. Like many other phenomena in life, Pareto's law suggests at least an 80:20 split, if not more. That's 80% sales and 20% product or technology. (If you've not heard of Pareto's Law before, check out the 'time management' section in Recommended Reading – you will not regret it.) You do have to understand the product and technology but it is much more than features and functions that he had to sell to the prospective customer.

As one of my interviewees Michael Townsend for the book put it: the product is merely a backdrop to the value proposition.

What I love about presales is that your peers are so willing to help you, and you hear all these war stories that open your eyes to new perspectives. Michael continues his own story by sharing what he also found surprising. He joined Egnyte as the presales manager from a customer of theirs. Clearly, he had a depth of knowledge about the product, having seen it in action and the realised benefits. "But", he added, "when you work as part of a team in a software house as opposed to a customer, you will find that you will be at the forefront of innovation": you have to keep up with the most advanced technologies, use cases, and customer visions.

To the surprise-factor list, I would like to add creativity. To be more specific, creativity in a sense that you create a lot of information documents. These could include architecture diagrams, process flows, and last but not least, sales proposals. I also mean creativity in a sense of daring to create new solutions and make sense of complex data by creating connections between entities.

To help with "writer's block" or a dreaded "blank canvas" I would encourage you to start your intellectually demanding document creation assignment with simple creativity exercise. Take a piece of paper, a pen, and start drawing a circle. Change hands – this will activate the other side of your brain – and draw another circle. Repeat. Try changing the direction of movement; draw a circle counter clockwise or vice versa. Now start the circular movement from a different starting point, e.g. bottom or top of the circle. After a couple of minutes, or when you feel you are done, colour in some of the shapes as if it were a colouring book.

Figure 5: After making marks on a piece of paper it is easier to tackle an important and challenging writing task. This simple creativity exercise wakes up both sides of your brain and defeats the blank canvas feeling. Draw circles of varying sizes, repeat with both hands; after a couple of minutes of drawing, it is much easier to start your main writing task!

The picture you create will not be perfect; the point is to get going. To send your mind a message through your body that says: You can create. You can do this. Then, get on with your real work.

More resources to explore on...

...creativity – a skill to be learned and nourished:
[Book with theory and practice] InGenius: A Crash Course on Creativity by Tina Seelig. Check out this and other books by her at http://www.tinaseelig.com/books.html.
[Book] Breath for the Bones, Art, Imagination and Spirit: A Reflection of Creativity and Faith, https://www.lucishaw.com/books_featured.html
[Book about God and science but also about creativity] God in the lab by Ruth M Bancewicz: https://www.faraday.cam.ac.uk/about/people/dr-ruth-bancewicz/. This blog post by her is a good start of discussion: https://www.faraday.cam.ac.uk/churches/church-resources/posts/what-makes-us-creative/

...time management, productivity and prioritisation:
[Method and theory] Pareto's Law says that you get 80% of

your results from 20% of your work: https://www.forbes.com/sites/kevinkruse/2016/03/07/80-20-rule/. If you would like scientific proof and read more about the time vs cost conversation, this scientific paper is worth a peek: "[Nobel prize winner] Gary Becker's a Theory of the Allocation of Time" by Pierre-André Chiappori and Arthur Lewbel https://academic.oup.com/ej/article/125/583/410/5076992

[Book, infographic and method] 15 Secrets Successful People Know About Time Management: The Productivity Habits of 7 Billionaires, 13 Olympic Athletes, 29 Straight-A Students, and 239 Entrepreneurs by Kevin Kruse. This and other books at https://www.kevinkruse.com/books/. A summary of the book, with an infographic, is at https://www.forbes.com/sites/kevinkruse/2016/01/20/15-surprising-things-productive-people-do-differently/?sh=28cc9d9e44b2 and is aptly titled Ultra-productive people do these 15 things differently.

[Method] 4 Ds Of Effective Time Management, summarised e.g. on Forbes https://www.forbes.com/sites/bryancollinseurope/2018/06/14/effective-time-management/?sh=6f0f5a111938.

[Video] Figure out what your high priority tasks are: https://www.youtube.com/watch?v=n3kNlFMXslo&feature=youtu.be

[Task management tools] There are countless time & task management tools, but my favourites include Atlassian's Trello https://trello.com; and the humble sticky note (the paper version stuck on a wall). Time management is more about the process than technology, so focus on the intended outcome first, then the process and then the technical application.

[Scheduling tools] Scheduling tools include X.ai https://x.ai, with a bonus that you will get to work with Andrew or Amy, your personal AI robot. Other solutions include Calendly https://calendly.com and Vocus.io https://vocus.io/product/calendar and Calendar https://www.calendar.com.

[Outsourced service] Virtual assistants are Virtalent in the UK https://virtalent.com and Virtual Gurus in Canada https://thevirtualgurus.com.

[Way of life] Organising your life generally (see happiness later).

[Specific productively tools] These will differ from person to person. An application I couldn't live without is 1Password https://1password.com. It is a password management solution (there are others, of course, to choose from) and has saved me hours of work and a lot of headaches.

[Philosophical question] Does productivity increase happiness? Research (and common sense) suggests that living in the moment makes you happy. But does productivity have the same impact?

SUPPORTING THE SALESPERSON, AND THE SALES PROCESS

So far, we've built a picture of a presales consultant that is very similar to a superhero. But the role isn't all about being in the spotlight, high fives and chest bumps. Nevertheless, they are all fun, and having fun makes offices enjoyable: As my manager gave me a chest bump the whole team ended up laughing out loud – I must have been his first female report and he hadn't quite adjusted his actions to this new change yet!

When you are in a real-life presales consulting role, you will need a huge amount of courage, self-awareness and self-confidence, but you need to be very humble. After all, what your role is, at the heart of it, is to help close a sale. And when it comes to closing a sale, it is the salesperson, not you, who leads it.

It can be difficult to balance the powers of the two main characters, the salesperson and the presales consultant, if the roles are not well-defined and discussed openly. Once, when I joined a fast-growing software company as an experienced presales consultant, I met the company's leading salesperson. He pulled me to one side and asked if we could have a chat. I wasn't sure what to expect and complied. We found an empty office and talked. He'd seen me at the interview, confident and showing off my leadership qualities. He was worried I might be trying to take the lead in the sales process, thus compromising his role, and jeopardising the sale.

He was experienced enough to take the initiative to talk through difficult topics openly with everyone involved in the sales process. Throughout my tenure at the company, Peter was a mentor to me. I still remember the day when I received the phone call. I was in a taxi with another colleague in Spain, where we were growing our operations. Peter was the first colleague of mine to pass away, and again, the presales team was there for each other. Steve, who had passed the news to me, said very kindly as we were gathered in the office. "You are very lucky not to have lost anyone at work before this. It is never easy, but it is part of life."

Work is never just about work. I love how Shellye Archambeau, one of the few African American female Fortune 500 CEOs, puts it: "There is no work-life balance. There is only one you, and you bring your whole self to everywhere you go." She explains how she is always a CEO, a woman, Fortune 15 Board Member, a wife, and a mother, wherever she goes. She has an extraordinary life story and I encourage you to read her book, "Unapologetically Ambitious". There's something for all of us to learn from in that book.

Understanding the wider context is one of the best things you can do to be better at your job and ultimately advance in your career. I've always had a soft spot for inspiring business books. My curiosity has allowed me to find new perspectives in what I do in each of my roles, and to speak with executives with insight and curiosity.

This holistic approach helps you both with self-awareness – a vital ingredient of traditional success – and organisational growth. Even if organisational growth is not something that you ponder in your daily activities, personal success should be big enough a driver for you to learn more about the organisational context that you are part of.

Figure 6: Holistic thinking includes two aspects: understanding your many roles in life and understanding the wider context of your responsibilities at work. As a successful presales consultant, it is vital that you understand the sales process from start to finish, and your expected contribution to it.

Take a moment to reflect the whole of you. What are the roles that you assume during the course of a day, a week, a month?

Further, who are the people at work that you help, and work with? What is the impact of your work?

One of the colloquial hesitations about joining the presales organisation from a post-sales role, is the fear of working with a horrible salesperson. I partially blame Hollywood films for this. In reality, it is very rare for a salesperson and a presales person not to get on. Like with any work relationship, you do have to put effort into good communication to avoid issues, and make sure to correct any misunderstandings as soon as possible. In the very unlikely event that the personalities constantly clash, you can always request from your manager to work with a different salesperson. There is no shame in that, either.

If you are already in a presales role, make sure to schedule time with your sales colleagues. Have a discussion about how you support each other, what your strengths are and make sure you cover each other's back at customer meetings. If you are feeling a bit more generous, it is not a bad idea to find out what makes the salesperson 'tick'. You can find out quite easily what they appreciate most just by asking. Some people really appreciate gifts, some kind words, others uninterrupted, focussed time. Take a look at the book '5 Love languages' under communication references to get you started.

What tends to happen in some companies, is that junior presales consultants are matched with senior salespeople, and vice versa. If this is the case in your company, take advantage of this gap and absorb the knowledge that the salesperson has. Especially when you are new to the role or the technology, or both, your salesperson will know more about the product than you do. That can be hard to handle emotionally, when you are meant to be the technical expert. The salesperson will most likely know a lot of customer stories as well and share her or his experience in front of the customer. Remember, that they also want to be seen as knowledgeable, and sometimes will feel under more pressure to have to 'prove' themselves.

When this happens in a customer meeting, simply thank the salesperson for sharing her insight, and move on. You may wish to clarify the technical aspect of the question after the meeting, with or without the salesperson as you see fit. Keeping a diary of all your learnings will make it easier for you to memorise the quotes from other customers, and soon you will internalise them and sharing those stories will become your second nature.

More resources to explore on...

...inspirational autobiographies:

[Book] Becoming by Michelle Obama
[Book] Between the stops by Sandi Toksvig
[Book] Unapologetically Ambitious by Shellye Archambeau
https://shellyearchambeau.com/books - yes, it is mentioned twice in the list of references (also in *'Beginning with the end in mind'*)

...communication:

[Book] Nonviolent communication: A Language of Life by Marshall B. Rosenberg

https://www.nonviolentcommunication.com/product/
nonviolent-communication-a-language-of-life-3rd-edition/
[Book and method] 5 Love Languages by Dr Gary Chapman is a book that I got as a wedding gift from my mum. If you are not sure you can cope with quite conservative ideas about marriage, or just want the learnings from the book, I would recommend reading a LinkedIn post by Fiona Brennan-Scott https://www.linkedin.com/pulse/whats-love-got-do-fiona-brennan-scott/. It is a short but informative article about how basic human desire (love) dictates the way we prefer to be treated and appreciated, at work.

TECHNICAL WIZARD A.K.A. CUSTOMER'S TRUSTED ADVISOR

If you have sales on one side, then on the other side of the coin of being great at presales you would have technology. Sometimes this is also known as being a trusted advisor (it is not quite the same thing, but it is splitting hairs). Research shows that only a fraction of salespeople are seen as trusted advisors to the customer. Whether that's right or wrong, most often that responsibility lies on the shoulders of the presales consultant. You should not take this information lightly.

The term 'trusted advisor' is an industry term, and one that most professionals aim for. But what does it actually mean? As the name suggests, it assumes a strong level of trust between the parties. Brené Brown, a transformative leader and professor, has had a huge impact on my thinking about trust. I come from a family where some things were never talked about. As I've discussed my life with friends and family members, I've discovered that most of the un-needed secrecy is the product of time. It is not just me that struggles with accepting the definition of trust that is so crucial to good living. Like so many of my generation, I have learnt later in life that building trust involves unravelling, and coming to terms with, and then dealing with things that are not the way you want them to be. Many of my parents' generation simply aren't used to sharing things that have any personal shame, however small, involved. So, when you are in the spotlight as the trusted advisor, be assured that it is a great place to be, but also full of responsibility that means dealing with negative issues. Being cognisant of generational, geographical, and other differences between you, your work friends and your customers helps you build a culture of trust that can take on the world. (Or, at the very least, close a sale – research suggests that people buy from people they can trust and feel like them).

Being a trusted advisor is "simple, but not easy" (courtesy of numerous presales consultants, but I am going to quote Pabel Martin who was the most recent person to tell me that). I am learning to play chess, and I discovered early on that it is the same as presales: simple, but not easy. It didn't take me long to know what the goal is (get the King), or what I need to do to get there (get your pieces and pawns in checkmate).

Figure 7: Chess and presales: simple, not easy.

Simply put, your task as a presales consultant is to build a solution that the customer wants to buy, and present it in such a way that they have no reason to say no. You do this by slowly building a "champion" within your customer. In other words, you win their trust. Building trust is not fast, and you do this by consistently building a better picture of the customer and empathising with them. Understanding your customer, their needs and what they want, you build a solution your company can deliver and make money on. At the same time, you tweak and re-tweak the solution you are recommending, and ensure that the solution matches the customer's requirements by encouraging a transparent conversation about what the customer's most important requirements are (the 'must-haves' vs the 'could haves'). For you to be a truly 'trusted' advisor for your customer, you need to adopt your customer's words and speak like them and share their values. All of that requires preparation, research, practice and authenticity.

More resources to explore on…

…personal leadership, trust, and finding your values:

[Book/meditative journal] The Art of Presales: Workbook: Your very own curiosity, creativity and happiness journal to explore the amazingness of your career in sales engineering by Dr Tuuli Bell (yes, that's me) https://www.amazon.co.uk/dp/B092P6WTX1

[Book, PDF, website, movement] Dare to Lead by Brené Brown. Her research on trust is summarised in a PDF at https://daretolead.brenebrown.com/wp-content/uploads/2018/10/BRAVING.pdf but if you have time, I would really recommend reading the book, too.

[Book, TED talk on YouTube, sales method] Start With Why by Simon Sinek https://simonsinek.com/product/start-with-why/ and https://www.youtube.com/watch?v=u4ZoJKF_VuA&vl=en

[Book and prioritisation method] 18 minutes by Peter Bregman https://bregmanpartners.com/books/18-minutes/

[Book and action-packed website] Six months to six figures by Peter Voogd https://peterjvoogd.com

[Book] Similar to Six months method, The 12 week year: Get More Done in 12 Weeks than Others Do in 12 Months by Brian Moran talks about prioritisation of time and energy https://12weekyear.com.

…learning about IT projects:

[Book] The Phoenix Project: A Novel About IT, DevOps, and Helping Your Business Win by Gene Kim, Kevin Behr, and George

Spafford https://itrevolution.com/the-phoenix-project/

[Framework and book] Flow Framework: https://flowframework.org/ and the related book https://projecttoproduct.org/ by Dr Mik Kersten

[Framework] Closely related to the FlowFramework, the SAFe framework also talks about value streams with some useful diagrams https://www.scaledagileframework.com/value-streams/

[Book] The DevOps handbook by Gene Kim, Jez Humble, Patrick Debois, and John Willis (https://itrevolution.com/the-devops-handbook/), and others by ITRevolution https://itrevolution.com/devops-books/.

QUALITIES OF A GREAT PRESALES CONSULTANT

In this chapter, we are discussing the ideal qualities for a presales consultant. Even though no one is a clone of each other, there are underlying similarities that connect the best performers. I do not think anyone is 'born' a top performer. Each of us have our own struggles. It is a mixture of listening to yourself – your mind and body – and working in harmony with yourself, your environment, and a greater cause that allow us to change ourselves.

That said, no person is an island. You will need a good support network, because when you stumble, your support network catches you and makes sure you never fall out of reach. Because we are all one person, it is good to ensure that you have both professional and personal support circles. I've always been building my professional network steadily throughout my career. This is very natural to me, and social network platforms such as LinkedIn make it easy to keep in touch and ask for help when you need it. You give and get back. My mum always says that life balances things out, meaning that you do not always give and receive from the same people. That's been great advice. It has helped me be more generous.

Before I became a mother, I didn't understand the acuteness of a personal support network. My family is in Finland, so I've never been expecting day-to-day help from them. However, after my daughter was born, I suffered, really suffered, from post-natal depression. I won't go into much detail, but I had some dark times. Years have passed and I am so grateful for having a family, but I still cry when thinking about some of the early months. I wish I would had more courage to ask for help, and leverage my personal network to get through it quicker.

Although everything in life, even the dark times, have a bright side, I can now appreciate why depression is classed as a disability in the UK. That has helped me respect the need for inclusivity at work. The society hasn't quite kept up with legislation and even now, you do not see many people talk about hidden disabilities. Those with visible disabilities make up only a tiny fraction of the workforce, and many remain out of work.

When life throws you into unexpected situations, what do you do? Nowadays, I do my best to pick myself up as soon as possible. I use a technique developed by Tamsin Napier-Munn, Founder RAW-talks academy. She taught me a simple technique where you count '3, 2, 1', and then make a physical move. If I need to complete a project I am passionate about under a tight deadline, I wake up early, count down and get out of bed. Building resilience is simple, but not easy. But it is well worth it.

More resources to explore on...

...change management – making anything happen:

[Book] Managing Change: Enquiry and Action by Nic Beech and Robert MacIntosh
[Method] Tamsin Napier-Munn (https://www.rawtalksacademy.com/meet-tamsin) taught me the "3-2-1: *physical action*" way of making anything happen: https://www.facebook.com/watch/?v=359753041812866

...understanding the impact of gender bias:

[Book] Reflections on Gender and Science by Evelyn Fox Keller
[Online test] Test Yourself for Hidden Bias: https://www.tolerance.org/professional-development/test-yourself-for-

hidden-bias

[Book] Invisible Women: Exposing Data Bias by Caroline Criado Perez

[Book] Why Women Will Save the Planet, edited by Friends of the Earth, Zed Books

[Infographic] UN infographic of impact and types of gender discrimination https://www.unwomen.org/en/digital-library/multimedia/2015/12/infographic-human-rights-women

[Podcast] Women in Sales podcast http://barbaragiamanco.com/women-in-sales-podcast/

[Community] BCS Women https://bcswomen.bcs.org/

[Community, conference] Slack group, mentorship community, and international conference by WomenTech https://www.womentech.net/women-tech-conference

[Framework, infographic] UN Sustainable development goal on gender equality https://sdgs.un.org/goals/goal5

WHAT MAKES A GOOD PRESALES CONSULTANT?

"Between stimulus and response there is a space. In that space is our power to choose our response. In our response lies our growth and our freedom."

- VIKTOR E. FRANKL, AUSTRIAN NEUROLOGIST, PSYCHIATRIST, PHILOSOPHER, AUTHOR, AND HOLOCAUST SURVIVOR

We've already touched on what your main goal as a presales consultant is. In short, you have to be able to influence the customer's perspective and explain the product and its value to the customer. How do you achieve this?

Mapping your personal development path into presales depends on your current circumstances, your background and experience. In the following diagram I've used a metaphor where your goal is depicted as the plant's growth and well-being. It will help you identify some of your future training requirements and should act as a reminder to always continue developing, wherever you are in your professional life.

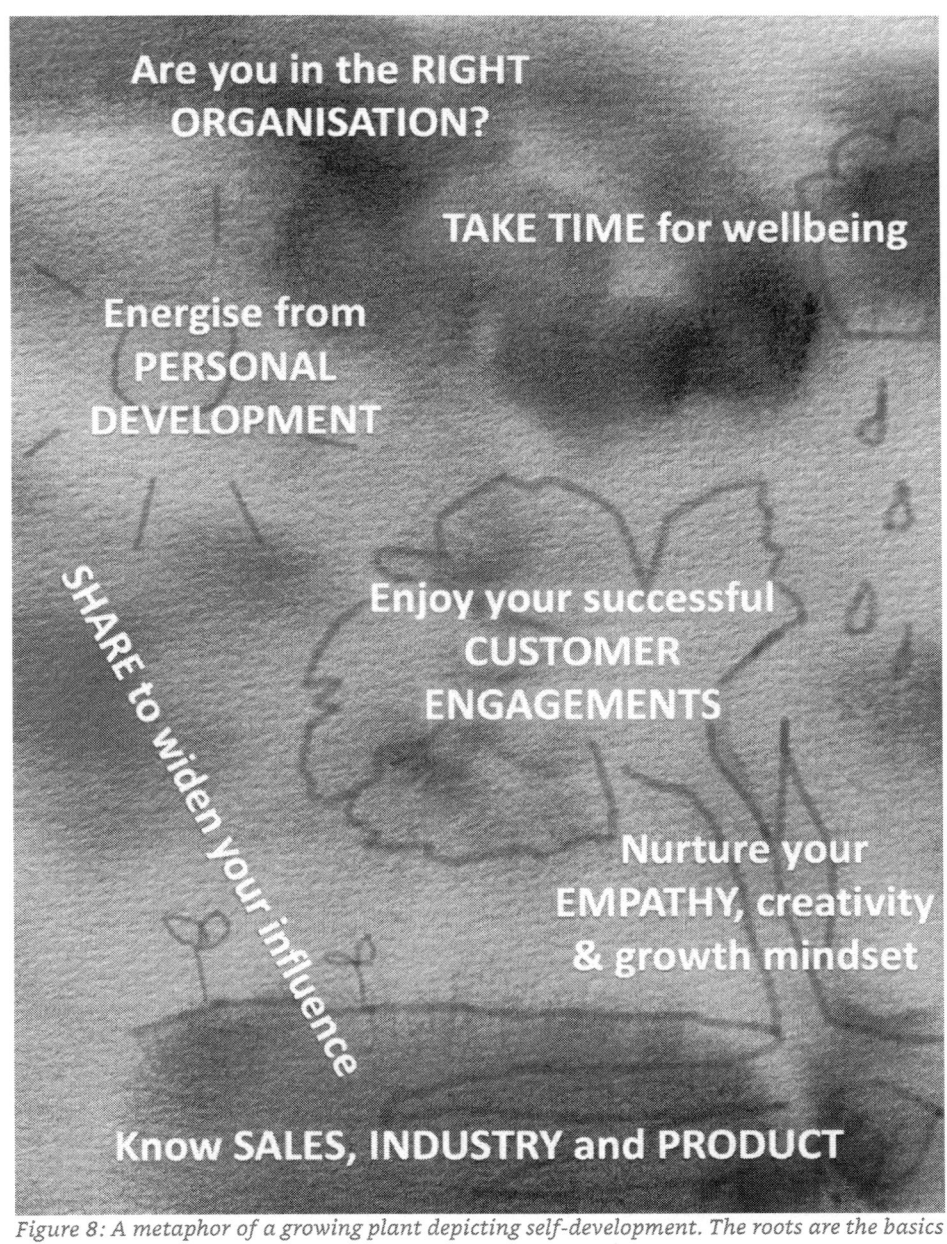

Are you in the RIGHT ORGANISATION?

TAKE TIME for wellbeing

Energise from PERSONAL DEVELOPMENT

SHARE to widen your influence

Enjoy your successful CUSTOMER ENGAGEMENTS

Nurture your EMPATHY, creativity & growth mindset

Know SALES, INDUSTRY and PRODUCT

Figure 8: A metaphor of a growing plant depicting self-development. The roots are the basics of presales: sales, product and industry knowledge. The flower of the plant depicts what other can see and appreciate: your successful customer engagements and sales.

To be able to grow the plant, you need strong roots. The roots are the basics of presales: sales, product and industry knowledge. For sustainable growth, the stem of the plant needs to be sturdy and flexible: your internal mindset should be open to empathy, creativity and growth. The flower of the plant depicts what other can see and appreciate: your successful customer engagements and sales.

A plant will need constant caretaking, and the same applies to your career. So that you can continue to grow, you need energy from personal development, "the Sun". You need to take time off for your own well-being; "the rain" that helps the plant to flourish. The right organisation, your environment, can make or break your career. As the name suggests, you cannot directly influence an environment, or the company that you work for: it is a shared responsibility. Sometimes, you will want to move to another company to be able to continue your growth.

Finally, your long-term goal as a diligent gardener might be to create a whole field of flowers and plants for everyone to enjoy. See the new seedlings, starting to grow and multiply. These represent the knowledge and wisdom that you share with others, to benefit your organisation and beyond.

To summarise, the top 10 qualities you should seek to become great at presales are:

1. Sales and persuasion skills
2. Product & technology knowledge
3. Industry experience
4. Growth mindset (*i.e.* happy to change your old habits and learn new ones)
5. Empathy
6. Creative skills (*i.e.* the ability to create)
7. Confidence and self-awareness
8. Resolute in prioritising your own well-being
9. Happy to take calculated risks
10. Communication

More resources to explore on...

...staying healthy (so you can live to do great things):

[Book] Gut: the inside story of our body's most under-rated organ by Giulia Enders (Author), David Shaw (Translator)
[Book] WomanCode: Perfect Your Cycle, Amplify Your Fertility, Supercharge Your Sex Drive, and Become a Power Source by Alisa Vitti

...developing your thinking:

[Book] Thinking, Fast and Slow by Daniel Kahneman
[Book] Good Thinking: Seven Powerful Ideas That Influence the Way We Think by Denise D. Cummins

WHY ARE SOME PEOPLE NATURALLY GOOD AT PRESALES?

You may already have met a great presales consultant. You admire the way she or he presents with confidence and always says the right thing. They would close sale after sale, receive great customer feedback. They're a great person to work with yet display authority.

Confidence doesn't come naturally. It may seem that confidence is an innate ability that you either have or you do not. I believe that anyone can learn anything. Yes, we all have personal preferences and interests. And that is why the world is such a wonderful place: different people have changed the world in different ways and continue to do so. Confidence grows as we can do things that we are good at and we like. Confidence grows our ability to strengthen our skills. A stronger skillset in turn grows our confidence. As we've discovered, successful presales consultants require a number of skills, namely sales skills with technical knowledge. When you have a strong technical skillset, you might be very confident in your abilities when deploying a technical solution. However, in new situations such as demonstrating platforms capabilities to a now prospect, you might find that your confidence level drops. Even if the technical skills required are the same, the dynamics of the participants are different.

Figure 9: There is a positive feedback loop between a person's confidence and skillset. The more confident you become, the easier it is to learn a skill. The more skilled you are, the more confident you become.

One of my interviewees explained to me how he found 'confidence' as one of the most challenging aspects in training technical people to support presales activities. In our discussions, he reflected that it might be a case of re-framing the request. Presales "selling" is really helping the customer make the right buying decision. Technical consultants have a vast amount of technical expertise, and they could leverage their project experience in sales situations. A one-to-one discussion before a prospect demonstration gives a morale boost for both the salesperson and the (temporary) presales consultant. It lifts some of the anxiety attached to a "sales call".

Along with confidence, empathy is a skill that may come more naturally to some than others. Empathy is a key part of emotional intelligence and is in high demand in our digitalised world. Empathising is much more energy-consuming than you might first think. It needs a deep level of maturity and trust. You have had to empathise a lot in your role already, whether you are in product management, support or professional services. You have had to think about user journeys, analyse requirements or decide if a new feature request is worth developing this quarter. Think back to the last time you spoke with a user or a customer. What was their feedback about your solution? The user would most likely have specific use cases and include not only their feedback but comments from their colleagues. Empathising is understanding the customer's viewpoint of the world. It includes their role and responsibilities at work, but also that of their colleagues and their families. Empathetic presales consultants come across as genuine, authentic professionals who live in harmony and work with integrity.

Skills that are seen as easier to "acquire" include strong communication skills, both written and spoken. If you think that communication is one of your core strengths, you will be able to advance in presales quickly. Effective communication includes body language, too. At university, I took my first classes in body language and I have since found its learnings useful in many situations. One of my favourite learnings was to start leaning forward if I noticed I was getting bored in a meeting. Leaning forward sends your body a signal that you are interested in what you are learning, and I use that to this day. Of course, your body leans forward 'automatically' in intrinsically interesting situations, so do not read this cue as someone getting bored when you speak! Most of us 'speak body language' without noticing and leaning forward can be interpreted as increased interest.

Finally, I would like to include creativity as a 'hidden talent' of successful presales consultants. For many of us in the technology industry, creativity is seen as an impediment to succeeding in 'cold' sales careers. However, it could not be farther away from the truth. Your inner creativity will help you tackle challenging situations and find 'creative compromises' in negotiations.

SELF-AWARENESS: DO YOU KNOW YOURSELF?

Empathy goes hand in hand with self-awareness.

Self-awareness is about being able to analyse your own being, ways of reacting, and thinking. Understanding how and why you react in certain ways (*e.g.* why you get anxious when giving a presentation) helps you get curious about your feelings rather than overwhelmed by them. At the end of the chapter, there are a few resources including videos that explain how the brain makes us behave in a certain way, helping you analyse your reactions to situations.

A quick and effective self-awareness 'pause button' is to take a deep breath. When you feel that your body reacts to a situation with a "fight, flight or freeze" response: pause, and breath in and out. Within moments, you will feel more relaxed and able to handle the situation with less negative emotion, and ultimately have a better outcome in the situation you are in.

Even if you are with a customer when this happens, it pays to pause, take a break from speaking for a moment or two. Your customer may feel compelled to fill the silence, which you should welcome with gratitude. You never know what the other person really thinks unless they share it with you.

Therapists use a method of connecting your body's physical and emotional states to help you find the right emotional response to a trigger. Sometimes, we as humans tend to react disproportionally to a trivial situation. For example, I get very angry inside, and sometimes noticeably so on the outside, when I see women laughed at, talked over or ignored. I will never accept this is a trivial situation, but it gives you an idea of a trigger-response mechanism. The reason I find it hard to control my emotions about it is because of my experiences of gender inequality and unfairness.

The good news is that you can align your mental and physical states to better control your outward emotional response in a similar situation in the future. Try to listen to your body's signals when you are feeling anxious; really get curious about what's going on in your body. You might feel your heart rate getting faster or a feel a sensation of heat or tightness in your body. When your body starts to react in a certain way again, it is a trigger for you to pay extra attention to how you react on the outside. Do you start defending yourself verbally or through body language? Do you start shouting or walk away?

The way you appear on the outside will depend much on your self-awareness. Self-awareness takes practice but comes more naturally for some more than others. Self-awareness doesn't mean that you shut off your emotions but rather become curious about them. Celebrating the range of emotions from joy to sadness and anger to hope is what makes humans human. When you understand your emotions better, you will be able to live and work a much more fulfilling life.

Daily meditation or prayer can help you reflect on your day and help 'control' your fight, flight, or freeze response in the future. If spiritual practice isn't for you, I suggest that you breath deeply, in and out ten times, a couple of times a week (or per day, if you can). Breath in through the nose, out through the mouth. Feel your body expand as you breath in, and contract as you breath out. Just be in the moment and enjoy the flow of your breath.

More resources to explore on...

...self-awareness and controlling your emotional reactions

[Video] Dr Daniel Siegel presenting a hand model of the brain on Flight, fight, freeze response and how to cope in difficult situations https://www.youtube.com/watch?v=gm9CIJ74Oxw

[Video] Understanding what is going on in your brain when you find yourself in a difficult situation: https://www.youtube.com/watch?v=eVhWwciaqOE

[Personality test] Find out your personality in an online test, by answering 10 multiple choice questions. The platform gives you the opportunity to validate your perceived personality with others, too. You will need to register but it only takes a few moments: https://innerworks.me/

[Personality platform] CrystalKnows https://www.crystalknows.com integrates with LinkedIn and the platform's AI categorises and analyses anyone's profile (and even gives you personalised selling tips).

[Article] Decision-making goes hand-in-hand with emotions: https://www.smashingmagazine.com/2019/02/human-decision-making/

[Article] Creating a space between a stimulus (a difficult situation) and your reaction: an article inspired by Viktor Emil Frankl who was an Austrian neurologist, psychiatrist, philosopher, author, and Holocaust survivor: https://www.forbes.com/sites/forbescoachescouncil/2019/10/02/be-a-better-leader-by-creating-space-between-stimulus-and-response/?sh=5c1017562feb

[Book] Interpersonal Networks in Organizations: Cognition, Personality, Dynamics, and Culture by Martin Kilduff and David Krackhardt is a very academic book which talks about the importance of self-awareness as a success factor in life https://www.cambridge.org/core/books/interpersonal-networks-in-organizations/37EAF702397220E72882BD5480D4928C

STORY ABOUT IMPOSTER SYNDROME

Imposter syndrome is one where the person thinks that they are a fake, not worthy of their achievements, and that the person fears that others will find out. It was only last year, a week or so after a deep discussion with a business coach, that I realised I had suffered from impostor syndrome for most of my life. It was a moment of awe, deep realisation, sadness, and relief at the same time. I felt ashamed; I thought that surely with my confidence that I display in all walks of life, it cannot be possible. Then, I reflected that I would compensate my fear by appearing over-confident. It had become my weapon of defence. The problem was that I, like everyone else in this world, are vulnerable whether we admit it or not. By always appearing confident, I would not let my vulnerability show.

I shared my imposter syndrome experience with a group of women in business shortly afterwards. I wasn't alone. Since then, I've noticed there's a growing number of executives who have been brave enough to share their story about imposter syndrome. I mentioned Shelley Archambeau earlier in the book, and I would like to recommend her book again.

If you are a man reading this book, imposter syndrome can be harder to admit due to existing social norms (which to the relief of humankind, are slowly changing). However, imposter syndrome is one that affects most people, both women and men. A healthy amount of confidence with a healthy amount of vulnerability is a balance worth pursuing.

PART 2: SALES

Methodologies, processes and marketing

A VERY SHORT INTRODUCTION TO SALES

You may have heard the expression of joining "the dark side". This has become part of presales' accepted terminology and refers to the act of moving from a technical team to a presales team. The 'dark side' is a reference of being part of a sales team, and it denotes the huge change in mindset. You are no longer motivated by a 'greater good of advancing technology' but the main driver is to close a commercial sale.

Whist I am not a particular fan of 'darkness', and believe in 'goodness', the oft-repeated term serves a useful purpose. A move from a technical role to presales indicates a complete change of processes, methodologies and ways of working. In this section, I intend to explain what sales is all about and how it applies to presales. After all, presales is part of the sales function, and the sooner you understand the basics, the easier the transition will be.

Figure 10: The move from a technical role to a sales role is sometimes referred to as 'joining the dark side'. This powerful terminology is used because of the huge change in mindset. For example, if you join a presales team from a software development, your main focus will change from creating the best user experience to helping the customer buy the right product.

More resources to explore on...

...understanding the humankind – a bit of philosophy to help put things into perspective during busy times:

[Book] Uncharted by Margaret Hefferman https://www.mheffernan.com. Future research at its best, which will change your thinking about today.
[Book] Sapiens: A brief history of Humankind by Yuval Noah Harari https://www.amazon.co.uk/dp/BOOK7ED54M/
[Book] Adapt and Thrive: The Sustainable Revolution by Peter McManners http://petermcmanners.com. This could belong to the "climate change and sustainability" section due to its content. However, it is a book that will change the way you look at life and appreciate the need for changes within business and society as a whole.

SALES METHODOLOGIES

We live in a world dominated by processes and structures, and sales is no different. Whoever claimed sales as "fluffy" or "unpredictable" certainly never worked in sales. Ask anyone in sales, and they will tell you all about metrics, KPIs (key performance indicators), close rates, opportunity percentages, and sales methodologies. And in the same breath (if they possess an Olympic-swimmer level lung capacity), they will tell you why all the metrics and numbers are a guess and no-one can predict the future.

Indeed, whilst being able to read the future would be a great party-trick, sales forecasting is as accurate as future predictions in general. You can improve the guess (of, say, how likely a sale is to close) by collecting and analysing lots of data, but that's always based on past performance. As economists, the greatest believers in prediction and future studies, put it: "past performance is no guarantee of future results".

Nevertheless, sales methodologies are designed to predict the future as well as they can, and it is not my job to challenge them. Sales methodologies are to selling a bit like Agile or ITIL are for developers or service managers. Sales methodologies give guidance what to consider when selling.

MEDDICC, a sales methodology, covers the basic components of a sales cycle. The methodology is widely adopted in technology sales but can be used in any industry. MEDDICC stands for 'metrics, economic buyer, decision criteria, decision process, identify pain, competition and champion'. In the next section, I'll show an example sales process where MEDDICC is used as the sales methodology.

You might come across other methodologies where you work, such as SPIN (situation, problem, implication, need-pay off), Sandler, Customer-centric selling, BANT (budget, authority, needs, timeline), Solution selling, or Challenger sale. Quite often, a new sales methodology is adopted when a sales team isn't performing, or when a new sales manager joins the team.

Knowing a sales methodology doesn't magically make you a great salesperson but it does help those who are starting out in sales. Sales methodologies give ideas about what information to seek when speaking with prospective customers. This information probing and deciding if a customer is a good fit or not, is called 'discovery' or 'qualification'.

Sales methodologies also give a shared vocabulary for sales teams when they are discussing an on-going sale. This mostly happens during weekly sales meetings and quarterly business reviews (QBRs) where sales managers ask for updates about deal closure plans. These team-based events are vital for peer support, too, and salespeople can ask for fresh ideas from their peers and share their experiences.

More resources to explore on...

...sales methodologies:

[E-book] The State of Sales Methodologies in B2B SaaS by MetaCX & Revenue Collective https://metacx.live.e3cms.net/wp-content/uploads/2020/10/The-State-of-Sales-Methodologies-MetaCX-Report.pdf
[Book] MEDDICC: The ultimate guide to staying one step ahead in the complex sale by Andy Whyte https://meddicc.com/product/meddicc-book/
[Book] The Challenger Sale: How To Take Control of the Customer

Conversation by Matthew Dixon, Brent Adamson https://www.hive.co.uk/Product/Matthew-Dixon/The-Challenger-Sale--How-To-Take-Control-of-the-Customer-Conversation/14082778

SALES PROCESS

Understanding the sales process has been quoted the one of the most important responsibilities of presales consultants. It is a bit like understanding any wider context, becoming part of you as you have more experience. For example, if you know the basics of cooking, you have the imagination, knowledge and confidence to alter recipes if needed. Running out of the everyday staple of herbs de Provence is no issue if there's a thyme bush in the back garden (trust me, this works).

A sales process follows each prospect from the beginning to the end. Roughly, the process has three parts:

1. Attract a prospective customer who has a need, to view your product or service.
2. Convert the prospect into a paying customer; or 'sell' the product.
3. Ensure the customer is happy and buys again from you; to 'retain' the customer.

Going back to my chocolate purchase example from the very beginning:

1. I needed chocolate to impress a customer and headed over to view chocolates on offer in Hotel Chocolat that was conveniently located at the train station.
2. The kind and efficient sales assistant queried my requirements and found the right items for purchase and took a payment.
3. The whole experience was very pleasant. The chocolates did their job by making my customer happy, and I have become a re-

peat customer. Just to be on the safe side, the company also sends chocolate brochures (without the chocolate, sadly) to my home address.

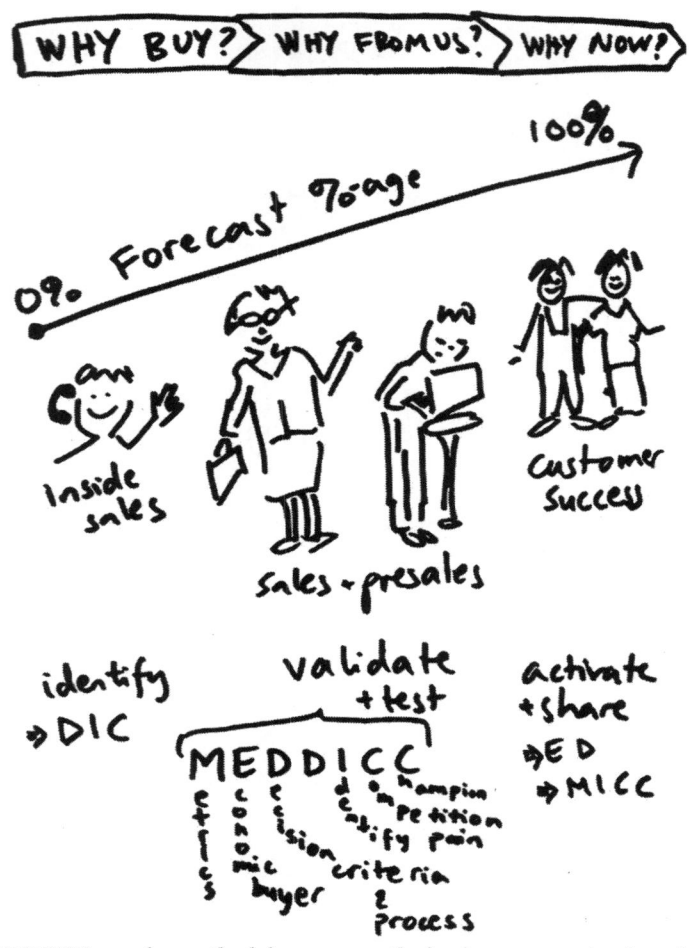

Figure 11: MEDDICC, a sales methodology, covers the basic components of a sales cycle. The methodology is widely adopted in technology sales, but there are others, such as SPIN or Challenger sale. MEDDICC stands for 'metrics, economic buyer, decision criteria, decision process, identify pain, competition and champion'.

A sales process includes a number of stages or phases. Figure 11 shows how naturally the forecast percentage (*i.e.* how likely the sale is to close) increases with each phase. The key internal and external stakeholders (or people) will change throughout. The first people to be in contact with a potential customer is the inside sales team, supported by marketing. As the sale matures and the prospect is qualified, the salesperson takes over the sale. The pre-sales person will support all technical elements of the sale. Once the deal is signed, there is an internal handover and the technical requirements will be handed over from presales to the customer success team.

The image highlights how one would adopt a MEDDICC methodology. First, DIC (decision criteria, identify pain and competition) are identified by the inside sales team. When the deal is handed to the sales team, all of MEDDICC (metrics, economic buyer, decision criteria, decision process, identify pain, competition and champion) are validated and tested. Then, ED (economic buyer, decision process) are activated *i.e.* the sale is completed and lots of people get involved (legal, sales operations, professional services and the rest of the customer success team, finance, and in some cases, the executive team). Finally, marketing team will want to share the customer story with the world, in particular MICC (metrics, identify pain, champion, competition).

This is a simplified version of a real-life sales process of traditional B2B sales environments. The model concentrates on the 'closing of the sale' which will be taught to salespeople across the world in sales training. In reality, salespeople will worry about where their next good lead (*i.e.* prospective client) comes from, and how they will achieve their quota (the 'number' that they need to hit to receive their much-appreciated bonuses). These worries sometimes result in miscommunications with the marketing and inside sales teams, whose main goal is to provide leads to the sales team.

Underperforming salespeople can sometimes easily be let go, but this rarely applies to presales consultants.

Similarly, salespeople will stay in contact with their customers after the sale is completed. Presales consultants are sometimes involved, but typically the 'technical advisory' role shifts to the professional services team after closing the sale. The presales team would re-engage the customer when there's a more concrete opportunity to grow the footprint of the solution, for example sell more software licences.

A more detailed example of a sales process is provided in the references section. The complete process could include process stages such as:

Find & Plan >>
Qualify & Discover >>
Influence & Choose >>
Go/No-Go >>
Validate & Propose >>
Negotiate >>
Close, Partner & Implement.

Processes are really fun to work with. If you are new to process analysis, spend extra time exploring each stage of the sales process at your company. For each of the stages, good first questions to consider are:

1. Objectives: What do we want to achieve?
2. Forecast %: If we achieve our objectives, what confidence should we give to this opportunity closing?
3. Actors: Who in our organisation is likely to be involved?
4. Activities: What activities/tasks do we expect to carry out?
5. MEDDICC: How can we use MEDDICC to continue qualification and ensure the quality of the opportunity?
6. Customer Verifiable Outcomes: What can we expect to get in return from our customer?
7. Internal Tools & Artifacts: What tools and artefacts are going to help?
8. Aligned KPIs, MBOs (management by objectives), OKRs (objectives and key results): How are we going to align, track, measure and report on our performance?

If you are not sure about something, ask your sales manager, or other people involved in the sales process. Sales process stages should be reviewed regularly, and sometimes asking a simple questions reveals a gap in the process, and you will be thanked for bringing up the inconsistency.

More resources to explore on...

...sales process:

[Process template] Detailed sales process example for you to download at https://docs.google.com/presentation/d/1KS6xmLFXzEb2JSfqrvAZnrI0ZaSyYlg0_aJCfWA1Ccc/edit?usp=sharing

SALES FROM A LEGAL PERSPECTIVE

As an inevitable part of sales, there are financial and legal elements that need to be negotiated. For many, these are regarded as separate processes and teams altogether, and referred to as the 'back office'. Listening to your legal and finance teams can be an eye-opening experience, and I would strongly encourage you to engage your legal and financial teams in conversations.

At a team level, integrating sales and legal teams by introducing each subject and way of working to each other will make things easier, and more fun.

I wanted to include a quote from Donna Sewell. She heads a UK-based legal business. I've had numerous conversations about sales-legal process alignment with her team, and there are so many commonalities. She says:

> *"Ineffective contracts can dramatically slow down the sales cycle and a company's revenue growth. LegalEdge works closely with sales teams to speed up deal completion: we create templates that are easy to understand and work for the business and their clients. We then help sales teams to negotiate and complete deals quickly and effectively within the company's risk parameters. And we create playbooks and train sales teams to understand their contracts and how to negotiate key terms more efficiently and effectively. By streamlining contracts and processes we make it*

easier to do business and empower sales teams to bring in revenue faster."

- DONNA SEWELL, CEO LEGALEDGE HTTPS://
WWW.LEGALEDGE.CO.UK/OUR-TEAM/DONNA-SEWELL/

More resources to explore on...

...negotiating (some would say that any discussion is a negotiation):

[Book by a hostage negotiator] Never Split the Difference: Negotiating as if Your Life Depended on It by Chris Voss and Tahl Raz https://info.blackswanltd.com/never-split-the-difference
[Method] "Empty the bucket method", courtesy of an old sales manager of mine. Ask your customer and partner(s) involved in the sale if there's *anything else* they can think of that might stop the sale from happening or slow it down. Write them down and tick them off one by one.
[Book] Effective negotiation: Effective negotiation by Ray Fells and Noa Sheer https://www.cambridge.org/gb/academic/subjects/management/management-general-interest/effective-negotiation-research-results-4th-edition?format=PB.

...introduction to finance:

[Book] Financial Intelligence, Revised Edition: A Manager's Guide to Knowing What the Numbers Really Mean by Karen Berman and Joe Knight. A great introduction to finance, for any leader in any industry.
[Book] Who cooked Adam Smith's dinner? by Katrine Marçal https://www.katrinemarcal.com_highlights the in-equalities of current economic metrics. The sequel, "Mother of Invention: How good ideas get ignored in an economy built for men" is published in June 2021.
[Financial metrics for climate change] The next era of circular economy and sustainable development will demand companies to include metrics on sustainability. The related law is being pre-

pared in the UK, and is mainly based on the framework of Financial Stability Board's (FSB) Task Force on Climate-related Financial Disclosures (TCFD). See e.g. https://www.gov.uk/government/ consultations/mandatory-climate-related-financial-disclosures-by-publicly-quoted-companies-large-private-companies-and-llps.

[Book, TED Talk, a way of managing cities] Doughnut Economics: Seven Ways to Think Like a 21st-Century Economist by Kate Raworth https://www.kateraworth.com/doughnut/

...finding joy and humour at work and in life:

[Book] "Research shows that adults fall off a humour cliff around age 23" so if you are older than that, read this book. "Humour, Seriously: Why Humour Is A Superpower At Work And In Life" by Jennifer Aaker and Naomi Bagdonas https:// www.humorseriously.com.

[Book and movement] Marie Kondo actually made me enjoy cleaning (to an extent), and appreciate a tidy environment on a different level. Find out more about the KonMari method through your choice of search engine. Books include Spark Joy https://www.amazon.co.uk/Spark-Joy-Illustrated-Japanese-Tidying/dp/1785041029/_and The Life-Changing Magic of Tidying: A simple, effective way to banish clutter forever https://www.amazon.co.uk/Life-Changing-Magic-Tidying-effective-clutter/dp/0091955106. She's even written a picture book for children https://www.amazon.co.uk/Kiki-Jax-Life-Changing-Magic-Friendship/dp/1529032113 (also works as a summary for adults).

[Book] Happy Hour is 9 to 5: How to Love your Job, Love your Life, and Kick Butt at Work by Alexander Kjerulf

[Book] The Courage to be Happy: True Contentment Is Within Your Power by Ichiro Kishimi and Fumitake Koga

MARKETING FUNDAMENTALS

Marketing has changed drastically in the last couple of years, due to consumer habits, changes in values, and advancements in technology. The role of marketing will thus differ slightly between companies depending on their marketing maturity.

The goal of marketing is, generally speaking, to gain as many marketing qualified leads (MQLs) as possible. The marketing team sends the MQLs to the sales team to qualify into sales qualified leads (SQLs), and to close a sale successfully.

To view marketing only as 'an input' to the sales process is an understatement. However, in most B2B organisations, the interaction between marketing and sales is one-sided. A culture change is slowly happening where marketing and sales teams work more closely together, but there is still a cultural divide between the teams.

The opportunities for driving financial results through marketing are huge. There are many forms of marketing, such as email, mobile, content and social marketing.

Content marketing refers to creating useful content for potential buyers, and includes things like 'how-to' blogs posts and infographics. Content marketing is gold-dust for companies, and pre-sales consultants can be a great asset in creating timely, important pieces of work for marketing purposes.

I do not have statistics, but I would guess that many successful marketeers have a degree in psychology. Marketing theories are fascinating, and they are constantly evolving.

In the book "Exponential influence", it is suggested that we are competing for customers' attention, not only time. 'Triggers' help grab a person's attention, and they can be roughly categorised to the following:

1. Peer & Power triggers: examples of usage include gamification, social triggers, self-profiling badges;
2. Personal Pursuit: *e.g.* 'mystery', self-improvement, puzzle of the week;
3. Prairie Dog events: *e.g.* Covid, 'time to check out the competition';
4. Productivity triggers: *e.g.* save time, 'fast choice', offer; a default option for customers, mobile apps; and finally
5. Price triggers: *e.g.* save money, limited time offer, creating scarcity.

By receiving multiple triggers, consumers form a (new) digital habit, for instance start using a new product or phone app. It is notable, that whereas in 'real life' repetition is the key to forming a habit, in a digital world, repetition kills a digital habit. For example, if you receive a daily email blast with similar content, you will soon start ignoring those messages. However, if an app notification is shown in lieu of an email, the user will more easily pick up the phone to check the notification and open the app.

Using the right vocabulary is important in your messaging. In the book 'Words that change minds', Rose Charvet explain that once people are be profiled according to their tendencies, beliefs, and personalities, it is straightforward to target theirs, and no-one else's, attention to your product or service.

To help you start an exploratory conversation bridging marketing and sales, I am including my favourite resources in creating a safe space for true, transformative conversations that are based on trust.

More resources to explore on...

...expanding your influence (these powerful methods should only be used in an ethical way, careful not to create addiction to devices/ tools/ software):

[Book] Exponential influence by Adrian Ott. Summary: You are competing for customers' attention (not only time). Use multiple triggers to form a digital habit (though repetition kills a digital habit!)
[Book] Words that change minds by Rose Charvet. There's a great summary about the book at https://www.solutionsforresilience.com/words-that-change-minds/.

...creating a safe atmosphere for online and face to face meetings:

[Book] A book that has influenced my way of leading workshops forever (check out my video on preparing for workshops at https://www.tuulibell.com/values.html). Time to Think: Listening to Ignite the Human Mind by Nancy Kline https://www.timetothink.com/nancy-kline/
[Book] Looking for creative ideas to transform a physical space? Check out this highly visual book. Make Space: How to Set the Stage for Creative Collaboration by Scott Doorley and Scott Witthoft https://dschool.stanford.edu/resources/make-space-excerpts
[Book] The art of gathering: How we meet and why it matters by Priya Parker is undeniably a great resource for re-discovering meaningful gatherings, both social and work-related https://www.priyaparker.com/thebook

...sales tools (non-exhaustive list, it gives you ideas about different types available):

[Customer relation management (CRM) tools] Your sales team might use one of Salesforce, HubSpot, Freshworks CRM, Zoho CRM, Monday.com; or ITSM tools such as ServiceNow, Cherwell, Jira, or HaloITSM for example. Most likely you will be using the same software to update your conversations and meetings with customers.

[Presentation software] In addition to Microsoft PowerPoint and MacOS Keynote, there are more interactive options such as Miro https://miro.com/, Mural https://www.mural.co/, and Prezi https://prezi.com/. Opensource, heavy-coding options include Latex Beamer https://ctan.org/pkg/beamer.

[Marketing automation software] There are thousands of tools to choose from; these technologies are designed to drive more leads to your sales team through web, mobile and AR digital traffic. They work by inviting people to engage with content that is interesting to them, and then capturing the persons' details (either implicitly or explicitly). Examples include Factoreal https://www.factoreal.com, Marketo https://uk.marketo.com, Eloqua by Oracle https://www.oracle.com/uk/cx/marketing/automation/, Hubspot https://www.hubspot.com, and Customer.io https://customer.io.

PART 3: SHARING YOUR WISDOM

Creating sustainable practices

SUSTAINABLE PRESALES IS THE FUTURE OF PRESALES

Congratulations on finishing the first two parts of the book. I trust you have a much deeper appreciation for the role of a presales consultant; regardless of the number of years of experience.

In this last chapter of the book, I would like to push the typical boundaries of presales. At the time of writing, the UK is embracing sustainable living, and with that, sustainable business practices and circular economy. Upcoming laws will regulate plastic packaging taxation, enforce the disclosure of financial data on climate-related metrics and give consumers the 'right to repair' of electronic items to reduce electronic waste.

The future is ours to behold, to take care of, and to responsibly enjoy. As presales consultants, we need to ensure that the products and services we advise on are as ethical as possible. For our customers' peace of mind, it is imperative that we remain the trusted advisor and keep up to date with the relevant frameworks and legislation that applies to our customers. When challenged, we can explain and reason to our customers why we recommend a certain solution over another.

Similarly, when we listen to our customers, we get the opportunity to learn about their individual challenges. For instance, your customer might struggle to track their supplier chain for plastic packaging tax credits. Your solution may help them solve the problem, with some extra configuration required. In return for the additional work, you would be rewarded by being able to sell your configured solution to many other customers, too.

Environmentally sustainable businesses will have a long-term vision for their companies. This makes them financially more sustainable, too, making them an ideal client for any sales team.

At the risk of expanding this chapter's 'more resources' section, I would recommend exploring new leadership styles. "Be More Pirate" by Sam Conniff is a personal highlight. The book explains that many of the best pirates were women, and there was true equality between the genders, races, and all of humankind. You may be surprised to learn that pirates were in fact a force for good, and they were great at storytelling.

More resources to explore on…

…understanding climate change, and what we can do about it:

[Interactive infographic] A detail from the easy-to-understand, effective Ellen McArthur Foundation's infographic on circular economy https://kumu.io/ellenmacarthurfoundation/ educational-resources#circular-economy-educational-resources/ key-for-general-resources-map/butterfly-diagram
[Framework, infographic] UN Sustainable development goal on energy (think IT/ data energy usage) https://sdgs.un.org/goals/ goal7 and how technology impacts the goal of "Strengthen the means of implementation and revitalize the global partnership for sustainable development" https://sdgs.un.org/topics/ technology
[Good life goals] How we can all help UN Sustainable development goals become a reality https://www.goodlifegoals.org. Manuals, flashcards, emojis at https://sdghub.com/goodlifegoals/.
[UK government policy, PDF] UK Government's 10 point plan for green industrial revolution: https://www.gov.uk/government/ publications/the-ten-point-plan-for-a-green-industrial-revolution. A must-read if you are in a leadership role in a UK-op-

erating company, to stay ahead of future laws on sustainability.

[Reading list] Check out the recommended reading list, on pages 6-8 in IT and Environment (BCS Higher Education Qualification, level 6) https://www.bcs.org/media/3764/heq-pgd-ite-syllabus-old.pdf

[Research article] How to 'recycle' software. Towards a Circular Economy of Industrial Software written by Vladimir Kutscher *et al.* https://www.sciencedirect.com/science/article/pii/S2212827120303127

[Community] Green IT, a BCS specialist group https://www.bcs.org/membership/member-communities/green-it-specialist-group/

[Self-improvement website] Giki Zero for tracking and baselining your carbon footprint https://zero.giki.earth

[Conference] Collision (Canada) and WebSummit (Europe) for all things applied tech, including sustainability https://collisionconf.com/ and https://websummit.com/

[Climate friendly blockchain technology] NEAR is an opensource platform for decentralized applications – currently the only climate-neutral blockchain technology (as at May 2021) https://near.org/.

[Reading list, video, movement] Part of Facing Change collection, this list of highly readable resources is compiled by Paddy Loughman. I learnt about it via Sam Conniff's Be More Pirate newsletter (thank you both!). Google document is at: https://docs.google.com/document/d/1PbtEqTKBIhn7CEP5vGRIJfqRb9Qr03AcOvp--u4Xmkw/edit. Video about Facing Change is at https://www.youtube.com/watch?v=ZSZQMJg6Z-Y&t=7s.

...business ethics – similar to environment, this is a hugely growing topic:

[Book] Morality in the technological world: Knowledge as Duty by Lorenzo Magnani, Università degli Studi di Pavia, Italy.

[Self-assessment webpage and PDF] Assessment List for Trust-

worthy Artificial Intelligence (ALTAI) by European Commission https://ec.europa.eu/digital-single-market/en/news/assessment-list-trustworthy-artificial-intelligence-altai-self-assessment.
[Community] BCS specialist group ICT Ethics https://www.bcs.org/membership/member-communities/ict-ethics-specialist-group/.

...about positively disruptive leadership:

[Book and movement] Be More Pirate by Sam Conniff https://www.bemorepirate.com
[Book and management style you will want to adopt] Employees First, Customers Second: Turning Conventional Management Upside Down by Vineet Nayar
[Book] Accelerate by by Nicole Forsgren, Jez Humble & Gene Kim https://itrevolution.com/book/accelerate/
[Book and humble leadership] Lead with Respect: A Novel of Lean Practice by Michael Ballé and Freddy Ballé,
[Book and a transformative workload prioritisation method] Making Work Visible: Exposing Time Theft to Optimize Workflow by Dominica Degrandis https://ddegrandis.com/book/
[Book] Leadership lessons from the navy. Turn the Ship around: A true story of building leaders by breaking the rules by L. David Marquet and Stephen R Covey

UPDATING INTERNAL PROCESS DOCUMENTATION AND TOOLS

There is a quote by Priya Parker: "Never end with logistics". She refers to never finishing meetings with admin and information about what happens next. Her advice works well for books, too.

So, I will share a couple of lines about admin in this penultimate chapter.

A lot of the work as a presales consultant is knowledge work. That knowledge needs to be transferred throughout the sales process – from you to the salesperson to the customer and back again. Also, and particularly so, the sales-to-post-sales handover takes place at the end of the sales process. This handover is critical in terms of customer success.

Processing knowledge means processing a lot of data and information. As the presales consultant you are expected to take a lot of notes and log them on an internal system. Most likely, the system you will be logging the information on is a CRM (customer relations management) software tool.

Consider the CRM as your friend. Your relationship status will depend on how often you exchange information and how much time you spend together.

Completing information on the CRM might feel like a lot of admin, because it is, but trust me, it is worth it. Having an up-to-date CRM will help your sales manager forecast upcoming sales (so that she can report to the CEO who can report to the Board of your company).

The CRM will also give crucial information to the post-sales consulting team. If you are not sure what information is useful, ask the teams that will use the data: marketing, sales, partner management, post-sales consulting, support, resourcing, HR, CEO, even product and development teams. It is also worth finding out which fields in the CRM are integrated to other systems – it will help you understand the sales process at a higher level and make you a true presales superhero!

More resources to explore on...

...sales tools for virtual meetings & phone calls:

[Video meeting solutions] Anything from consumer-focussed tools such as FaceTime, Skype and WhatsApp video to Zoom, Microsoft Teams and Vidyo which are aimed at businesses.
[Cold-calling solutions] Your sales teams might use technologies like ConnectAndSell to increase the number of initial conversations https://connectandsell.com. Alternatives, albeit with different product features, include Aircall and SalesLoft amongst others.
[Transcription and phone analysis technology] Refract analyses sales conversations for coaching and professional development purposes https://www.refract.ai/. Similar technologies include Chorus https://www.chorus.ai, Marsview https://www.marsview.ai/, and Otter https://otter.ai/. Slightly differently, Rev https://www.rev.com/ offers automated captions for Zoom and human-verified transcription and translation services.
[Integrated platform analysis / AI technology] Gong captures information from phone calls, CRM, and other sources to give a more accurate overview than a standalone CRM: https://www.gong.io.

[Phone / AI technology] A more generic tool than Gong, Contexta360 is a speech and chat AI for big data and its technology can be used to understand pre-sale and post-sale conversations at a large scale https://contexta360.com.

...presales tools (in addition to the sales tools above):

[Presales operations] A comprehensive presales tool puts presales operations at the heart of sales. Check out Vivun, for example https://www.vivun.com, and Prelio https://www.preliotech.com.
[POC management] Success app, for example https://www.success.app.
[Demo automation] Creating automated demos is possible through e.g. Consensus https://www.goconsensus.com/how-it-works/
[Product feedback management] For collecting feedback from customers and making product decisions based on data. See Uservoice, for example: https://uservoice.com/.
[RFP management] Loopio, for example: https://loopio.com. Internal 'wiki's' or knowledge management software such as Atlassian Confluence (https://www.atlassian.com/software/confluence) can be used for the same.
[RFP security questionnaires] Specialised software for responding to security questions in RFPs: see e.g. https://www.rfpio.com/ or https://www.hypercomply.com

MAKING YOUR EFFORTS VISIBLE AND REUSABLE BY THE REST OF THE ORGANISATION

CEOs will know this fact without further research (although the research does exist): sharing information within a company increases organisational revenue. Sharing of information within a company is also known as 'organisational knowledge'. When self-promotion is done with the intention of helping increase organisational knowledge it is one of the best things that you can do as a presales consultant.

In fact, sharing and collaboration is such an important aspect of the work, that in some organisations sharing information is one of the criteria for promotions and pay reviews.

Why is sharing so difficult? That's quite a philosophical question and I do not have all the answers. We have to learn to share. Learning to share information can trigger a feeling of embarrassing: What information should I share? Will I feel that sharing information is useless if everyone knows it already?

I still remember writing my first blog post for our marketing team. I was fresh out of university, with almost nil experience of the industry. With encouragement from the marketing director, my blog post became very popular amongst readers. Fast-forward a few months and I spent a considerable amount of time writing content, which further increased my confidence levels. Writing blogs also allowed me to explore new ways of expression and creativity at work.

Sharing information is not necessarily a formal activity: it can take place in casual conversations with people within your team or in the wider organisation. Hybrid workplaces and flexible working patterns mean that even these one-to-one chats might be online more often than not. Find out where the discussions happen – instant messaging, document collaboration sites, *etc.*

Sometimes, though, you have a feeling that you have learnt something very special or connected information in a novel way. You realise that this discovery could have a profound impact on your company (or your team, the very least). In those moments, embracing your inner child is nothing to be ashamed of. Get curious about your learnings and share your excitement with your team – you will never know where it takes you!

More resources to explore on...

...communication and collaboration tools:

[Instant chat messaging] Slack is a great platform for internal and external chat. Others include Facebook messenger, WhatsApp or Discord https://discord.com (depending on your audience).
[Document collaboration] Depending on the other tools you are using, pick one that integrates well with your existing tech stack: from e.g. Google Drive https://drive.google.com/, Dropbox https://www.dropbox.com or Microsoft's OneDrive http://onedrive.live.com.
[Document management for large teams] Atlassian products https://www.atlassian.com are great for transparent business processes and document sharing and you might already be using some or all of them e.g. Trello, Confluence, or Jira. If you

have multiple document sources, tools such as Egnyte https://www.egnyte.com are very useful for governance and productivity.

…resources for developing presales techniques for pros:

[Book] Sales Fundamentals for Technical Specialists Kindle Edition, Janne Korhonen https://www.amazon.co.uk/dp/B072BWCSVD

[Book] Driving the Technical Sale: Winning over the technical influencers. Master the Evaluation process by Lance Knight https://www.amazon.com/Driving-Technical-Sale-influencers-Evaluation-ebook/dp/B01MTON5YO

[Book] The Six Habits of Highly Effective Sales Engineers by Chris White https://www.amazon.co.uk/dp/B07T2TCHNT/ (similar sounding to 7 Habits of Highly Effective People® by Stephen R. Covey but not the same https://www.franklincovey.com/the-7-habits/)

[Book] Demonstrating to Win!: The Indispensable Guide for Demonstrating Complex Products by Robert Riefstahl https://www.amazon.co.uk/Demonstrating-Win-Indispensable-Complex-Products-dp-0615477097/dp/0615477097/

[Book] Great Demo!: How To Create And Execute Stunning Software Demonstrations by Peter Cohan https://www.amazon.co.uk/Great-Demo-Stunning-Software-Demonstrations/dp/059534559X

[Book] Mastering Technical Sales: The Sales Engineer's Handbook by John Care and Aron Bohlig https://www.amazon.co.uk/Mastering-Technical-Sales-Technology-Management/dp/1596933399

[Website resource] My website https://www.tuulibell.com/presales.html is dedicated to ambitious presales consultants for continuous learning and development, especially on the subject of sustainability and circular economy.

THANKS

Throughout the writing of this book, I have received support from many individuals in the form of advice, comments, and above all, sharing stories. Thanks to technology (and a worldwide lockdown), I have been able to speak to people all over the world about presales, technology, and business. All these conversations have contributed to the contents of this book.

Daniel Woodward is thanked for helping with the book structure, Michael Townsend for sharing his professional development program and commenting on the manuscript, Pabel Martin for discussing the role of the presales consultant, and his personal learnings of the importance of understanding the wider context, Aaron Davies for authors' peer support, Nick Shanagher for business development discussions, Nick Hansell for encouragement, Oliver Quie for personality discussions, Gerry Hill for discussions on culture change and the importance of picking up the phone, Presales community and James Kaikis for the valuable connections and making the world's best presales consultants more connected.

Thank you to my early readers and book champions: Aaron Davies, Daniel Woodward, Michael Townsend, Toni Yates, and Avani Hall without whose feedback the book wouldn't be here.

I would like to extend my further thanks to Deepal Jain, Nick Klatt, Matt Ridley, Avani Hall, Kris Meulemans, Semir Jahic, Prem Ramachandran, Divas Kapur, Lance Knight, Vridhi Tuli, Wesley Coelho, Jeff Downs, Andy White, David Samuel, Stephen Porter, Laksh Ranganathan, Maciej Kawecki, Adam Godfrey, and Mark Jenner for valuable discussions.

Thank you Sally Blake and Rebecca Jackson at LegalEdge for explaining the legal side of sales, and Donna Sewell for providing text for the book. I would like to thank my customers, especially those who, during 2020, prompted me to write this book.

Thank you to Phil, Carolyn and Neelan: your support means so much to me. I would like to thank my early managers, colleagues and mentors who have influenced my thinking over the years: Joe, Gerd, Camilla, Rod and Simone.

Thank you to Jade and Jonna at FBCC and Salla at the Finnish Church in London for support. Thank you to my friends for support during this time, especially Leni, Hannah, Tiina, Harriet, Mel, Marzena, Kirsty, Heli, Susanna, Phil, Vix, Sophie, Inga and Chris.

I would like to thank all the readers of the Art of Presales series, especially those who bought my first workbook and shared their feedback. Your comments encouraged me to keep going and complete this book. Thank you Steve for sharing your picture with the book on Facebook, that made my day!

Thank you, my reader, for picking up this book.

Thank you to Matt and Louize at The Curious Lounge by providing the most excellent office space in Reading. I love your tagline "Reading's only Indie Business Lounge". Thank you to Toni, my amazing executive assistant.

Finally, I would like to say a huge 'thank you' to my loving family and relatives: Dave and Mari at home, the Bells and Glasse-Davies in Scotland, äiti, Laura, Helena, Frida, Tilda, Martti, Essi, Anton, mummu and Imme in Finland, isä in Namibia, and Anna & family in The Netherlands.

ABOUT THE AUTHOR

Dr Tuuli Bell

Dr Tuuli Bell is a technology and business transformation consultant whose mission is to solve the most challenging problems of her clients. As a principal consultant, she has extensive experience across organisational functions from IT, service management to technical sales, service delivery and executive offices.

Tuuli is also a published author, an illustrator, and an artist. For Tuuli, happiness is about embracing change, connecting with others on a human level, and communicating with the universe through visual art.

BOOKS IN THIS SERIES

The Art of Presales

Presales, also known as sales engineering, has attracted thousands of ambitious (read 'high-salaried') people who brave both technical and sales mastery. If you're one of them, this truly interactive and timely series is a must-have for your personal and professional development.

Dr Tuuli Bell, PhD, is a management consultant and a visual artist. As an external consultant, there's a pressure to provide immediate return on investment. She says: "I have been asked to create sales templates that could be used straight-away, write customer-specific documents that would be key to closing an on-going sale, and collate answers to hundreds of questions that could stop a sale from happening."

I knew I wanted to write a book, and help others discover this exciting and awarding career. But I needed more help and wanted to ensure that the advice in the books would benefit those who read it. I joined a community of presales consultants and received a warm welcome. Talking through what problem existed that the book could solve, it became increasingly clear that there's a lack of guidance for people who want to join a presales team, whether temporarily or permanently.

I'd seen this happen throughout my career, and increasingly in the past year: companies still wanted to grow but were hesitant to hire costly presales consultants. The companies then ended up asking anyone who is available, to help with documents, demonstrations and sales conversations that had a technical aspect. When the task is finished, or help no longer required, the helper is sent back to their normal work which is often post-sale consulting. The cycle then repeats itself during the next sale opportunity.

Generally there is little support, help or training, and the new team members are thrown to the deep-end with varying success. Not only is it a costly way for companies to do business, jeopardizing a sale, but also can hit the confidence of the employee if they fail in their task.

If you've ever been in a situation described above, this book series is for you. I believe that anyone, with the right tools, guidance, and an open mind, can be great at presales. I'm honoured to serve as your guide as we discover the art of presales together.

The Art Of Presales: Workbook: Your Very Own Curiosity, Creativity And Happiness Journal To Explore The Amazingness Of Your Career In Sales Engineering

Explore the wonderful world of presales in this easy-to-use, fun, yet deeply reflective, challenging, 'for-your-eyes-only' journal-style workbook. Plenty of space for your own writing, drawings and diagrams, the workbook offers a well constructed guide to navigate your current presales role.

A dedicated "career coach bot" section gives you an opportunity to visualise your future career, also giving tips based on your personality. If you're up to it, you'll be able explore your personal vision, values, and mission; and further compare them to your employer's. You may end up thinking about the meaning of life, so proceed with caution.

You can explore the workbook from the beginning to the end, or in your chosen, or random, order.

The perfect antidote to those many hours working on your laptop, there's something calming about putting your thoughts on a piece of paper. There are practical exercises to choose from, including: creating your own list of acronyms, spotting opportunities for improvement, and writing the corporate value proposition in your own words.

Enjoy!

ACRONYMS: SALES, ORGANISATION AND TECHNOLOGY RELATED

Acronyms are also available via the QR code above. The QR code takes you to https://www.tuulibell.com/art-of-presales-acronyms.html.

1POC – First point of contact
AI – Artificial intelligence
ALTAI - Assessment List for Trustworthy Artificial Intelligence
a.k.a. – Also known as
API – Application programming interface [software data exchange method]
AR – Augmented reality
B2B – Business-to-business [sales]
B2C – Business-to-consumer [sales]
BANT – Budget, authority, needs, timeframe [sales qualification method]
BCS – The British computing society, a chartered institute for IT

BDR – Business development representative
BPO – Business process off-shoring; business process outsourcing
BSM – Business service management
C2C – Cradle to cradle [sustainability / circular economy concept]
CDO – Chief diversity officer
CEO – Chief executive officer
CFO – Chief financial officer
CHRO – Chief human resources officer
CRM – Customer relationship management
CRM - Content resource management
CSF – Critical success factor
CSI – Continual service improvement
CRO – Chief revenue officer
CSRO – Chief security risk officer
D2C - Direct-to-consumer [sales]. *See also:* B2B, B2C, O2O
DOU – Document of understanding. *See also*: MOU
EBIT – Earnings before interest and taxes [margin]
EOL – End of life. Meaning the date after which product is no longer supported
ERP – Enterprise resource planning
ESG – Environmental, sustainability, governance [framework for companies]
ESM – Enterprise service management
FSB –Financial Stability Board
GBS – Global business services
GRI – Global reporting initiative [set of sustainability standards]
GRC – Governance, risk and compliance [policy/ process]
NDA – Non-disclosure agreement
HA – High availability [as applies to software/ data centre]
ICT – Information and communication technology [field of study]
INVEST – Independent, negotiable, valuable, estimable, small, testable [requirement]
IoT – Internet of things
IoRT – Internet of robotic things
ISO – International standards organisation
ITAM – Information technology asset management

ITIL – Sorry this isn't an acronym, but I thought you might look it up here. If you wonder where the word comes from, it used to be derived from IT Infrastructure Library but is "definitely not an acronym anymore". ITIL is a business and IT framework for companies, and the latest version is ITIL 4 (as at February 2021).

ITSM – IT service management

KPI – Key performance indicator

LCA – Lifecycle assessment [sustainability / circular economy methodology]

LLD – Low level design; low level documentation

MAC – Move add change

MBO – Management by objectives

MEDDICC – Metrics, economic buyer, decision criteria, decision process, identification of pain, champion and competition. Used in sales qualification.

MI – Management information

ML – Machine learning

MoSCoW – Must have, should have, could have, would have. A scoring method that shows how important a requirement is.

MOU – Memorandum of understanding [legal document]

MQL – Marketing qualified lead

MSP – Managed Service Provider

MTTR – Mean time to repair; mean time to recovery

MVP – Minimum viable product

NLG – Natural language generation

NLP – Natural language processing [technical term]

NLP – Neuro-linguisting programming [psychology term]

O2O - Online-to-offline [retail]. *See also:* B2C, D2C, B2B

OKR – Objectives and key results

OLA – Operational level agreement [internal agreement]

OOTB – Out of the box. *Also:* OOB

PCF – Pre-Approval Control Functions

PCR – Process change request

PRC – Project change request

PDP – Personal development plan

PDPDO – Plan, discover, prepare, deploy, operate

POC – Proof of concept
POT – Proof of technology
POV – Proof of value
PQQ – Pre-qualification questionnaire [part of procurement process]
QBR – Quarterly business review
QoS – Quality of service
RACI – Responsible, accountable, consulted, and informed
RFI – Request for information
RFP – Request for proposal
RFSP – Regulated financial service provider
RFT – Request for tender
RFX - Request for [something]
RIDAC – Risks, issues, decisions, actions, changes
RM – Resource model
RMA – Return material authorization
ROI – Return on investment
RPA – Robotic process automation
SaaS – Service as a software
SAFe – Scaled agile framework
SAM – Software asset management
SD – Service desk
SDG – [UN] Sustainable development goal
SDLC – Systems development lifecycle
SDR – Sales development representative [a sales person]
SFDC - Salesforce [software]
SFP – Strategic financial plan
SIAM – Service integration and management
SIAM - security, infrastructure, asset management
SID – Shared information data [model]
SIEM – service, incident, event management
SLA – Service level agreement (many OLAs)
SME – Subject matter expert
SME – Small-to-medium enterprises [segment of companies; smaller than 'enterprises']
SOW – Statement of work [legal document]

SPIN - Situation, problem, implication, need-pay off [sales methodology]

SQL – Sales qualified lead (a subset of MQLs: marketing qualified leads)

SQL - Structured query language (a database)

SRM – Service request management

SW – Software

SWOT – Strengths, weaknesses, opportunities, threats

TCFD – Task force on climate-related financial disclosures. *See also:* FSB

TLA – Three letter acronym

TOI – Transfer of information

TQM – Total quality management

VR – Virtual reality

WORDS EXPLAINED

Cross-sell (or: X-sell) – The activity of selling complementary products or services to an existing client; often from a different product stack. *See also*: Upsell

The dark side - refers to crossing the line from a technical team to a sales team (of which presales is part).

Demo – a live presentation of software to a prospect. Typically (but not always) you will know what the prospect needs from the solution beforehand and are able to customise the presentation accordingly.

ITIL – a business and IT framework for companies. The latest version is ITIL 4 (as at February 2021).

A presales consultant – a person in the sales team that ensures the alignment of technical and fiscal proposals, and acts as a trusted advisor for the customer. Also known as sales engineer; presales architect; solutions consultant; solutions architect; sales support engineer; SE; SC; technical sales consultant; trusted advisor; and thought leader.

Solution – encompasses the entire value proposition: tool/technology, professional (implementation) services and training, for example.

Thought leader – A person who leads the general discussion in her or his field, for example by sharing their vision at panels, webinars and other networking and discussion events. They will often have published blog posts, white papers or eBooks on the subject, and are recognised by their peers as a knowledgeable subject matter expert.

Tool – A technical product that your company sells. This could either be software, where you sell licences, or hardware, where you sell boxes. It is part of the overall solution that you offer to your customers. Other parts of the solution you are selling may include enablement or training, professional services, financial services, or other complementary (upsell) products.

Upsell – The activity of selling additional products or services to a new or existing client. *See also*: Cross-sell

Value proposition – A corporate-mandated sentence or paragraph about how your company's products and solutions help a typical customer. You will want to learn this word to word by repetition (fake it 'till you make it) and then change it slightly so it feels your own.

Value stream - A value stream is a set of steps that create something that a customer wants to buy. That set of steps could include building, coding, selling, and most importantly, moving information.

CLOSING REMARKS

What I love about presales is that learning is part of the role. Figure 12 summarises the main learnings from the book in a simple but non-exhaustive manner. If you are still hungry for more information, check out the 'More resources to explore' sections at the end of each chapter and pick the ones that catch your attention. If any of the links do not work for whatever reason, please email me directly at tuuli.bell@tuulibell.com and I will do my best to help you.

I wish to celebrate the importance of communities and life-long learning; and encourage you to seek your own community, your (digital) tribe, where you feel safe to learn and to be vulnerable.

Through this book, I hope to have inspired you to do your best work as a presales consultant.

I am incredibly grateful to the many people that have mentored, coached, and supported me in my career. Thank you to you all.

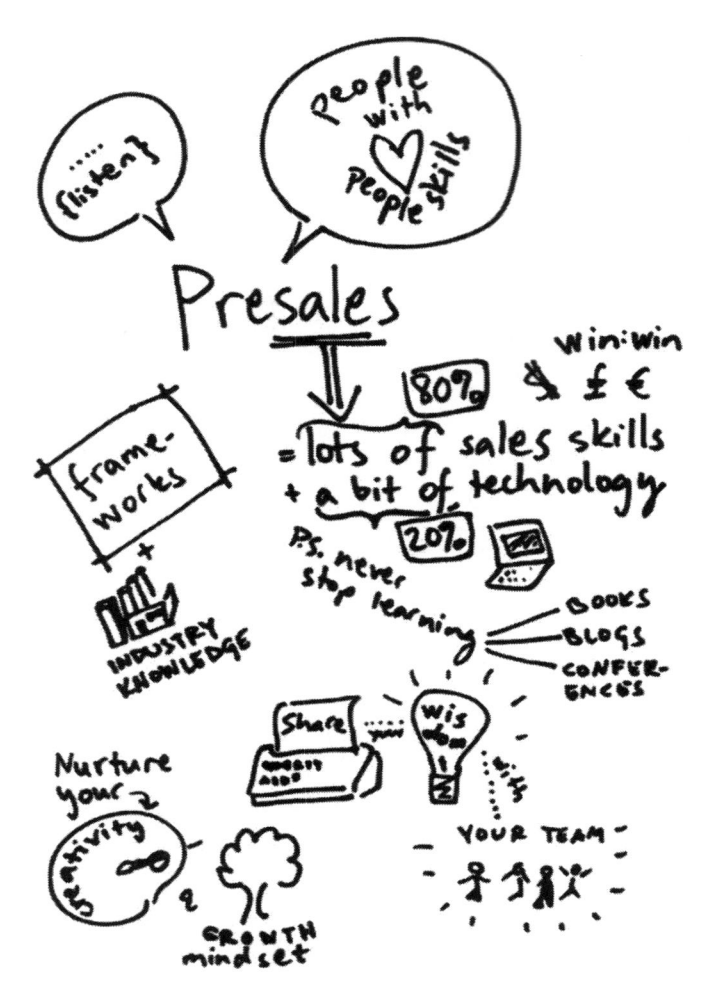

Figure 12: To summarise, presales is mostly about sales skills, with some technical skills. It is paramount to take care of your wellbeing through nurturing what is important to you, and to maintain a growth mindset. Share your wisdom with your team and the wider community to help others around you.

More resources to explore on...

...presales communities, and about community building:

[Community and podcast] Presales Collective for presales consultants of all abilities and from all continents: https://www.presalescollective.com/. Podcast is at https://www.presalescollective.com/podcast; also on Clubhouse.

[Community] WISE: Women in Solution Excellence, part of the Presales Collective https://www.presalescollective.com/wise.

[Community] BCS, the Chartered Institute for IT is a UK-based organisation with lots of different specialist groups to choose from: https://www.bcs.org/membership/member-communities/

[Book] Understanding and building communities: Hacking Communities by Laís de Oliveira https://hackingcommunities.com/. The most interesting take-away for me was how wide-spread the issue of lack of communities is in 'modern' societies. This lack of community-feel results in loneliness, depression, and lack of meaning for a large proportion of people. On a positive note, anyone can start building a community, whether virtual or physical; and positively influence the wider society through cohesive support networks.

Printed in Poland
by Amazon Fulfillment
Poland Sp. z o.o., Wrocław

20692977R00058